The
BLACK DEATH

The BLACK DEATH

Tom McGowen

A First Book

———•✦•———

Franklin Watts
A Division of Grolier Publishing
New York / Chicago / London / Toronto / Sydney
Danbury, Connecticut

FOR TIFFANY

Cover illustration by Stephen Savage

Photographs copyright ©: Art Resource, NY: pp. 2 (Giraudon), 25, 54 (both Scala), 32 (Erich Lessing); North Wind Picture Archives: pp. 8, 12, 18, 40, 42; The Bettmann Archive: pp. 10, 15, 20, 34, 37, 38, 45, 48; Archive Photos: p. 17; New York Public Library Picture Collection: pp. 26, 28, 30, 50, 52.

Library of Congress Cataloging-in-Publication Data

McGowen, Tom.
 The black death / by Tom McGowen.
  p. cm. — (A First book)
 Includes bibliographical references and index.
 ISBN 0-531-20199-6 (lib. bdg.)
 1. Black death — History — Juvenile literature. [1. Black death — History
2. Plague — History.] I. Title. II. Series.
 RC172.M34 1995
 614.5'732'009 — dc20   95-2122
                                                                           CIP
                                                                           AC

CONTENTS

I
THE RISE OF THE BLACK DEATH

II
THE BLACK DEATH COMES TO EUROPE

III
THE SPREAD OF THE BLACK DEATH

The
BLACK DEATH

A MEDIEVAL MONGOL CAMP

THE RISE OF THE BLACK DEATH

In the year 1320, the vast Mongol Empire spread across most of Asia. It stretched from what is now Iraq, in the Near East, to Korea, in the Far East, and from southern Russia in the north to India in the south. The place where this great empire had begun was the Gobi Desert, a broad, windswept region of dry grassland, sand, and rock that lies where a part of southern Mongolia touches northern China. From here, early in the thirteenth century, the armies of Mongol horsemen had swept out to conquer the lands for thousands of miles around.

In the late 1320s a sickness broke out among the rats that infested one of the little communities in the Gobi. These rats began to die by the dozens, the scores, the hundreds. Fleas that had lived on the rats and fed on their blood sought new sources of food. Carrying the disease that had killed the rats, the fleas made their way to the nearest humans. Abruptly, people began to sicken and die.

The Gobi was the center of the empire, and almost every day, messengers on swift horses rode out of it into all the surrounding areas where the Mongols ruled. Now, many of these messengers carried rat fleas on their bodies as they rode off. Some of the messengers were dying by the time they reached their destinations. Within days, some of the people they had spoken with,

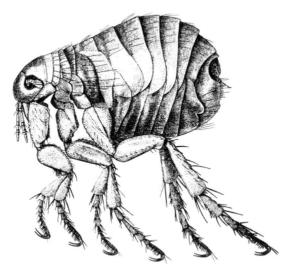

THE TINY FLEA (SHOWN HERE IN ENLARGED DETAIL) WAS THE MESSENGER OF DEATH FOR MILLIONS OF PEOPLE.

brought messages to, bought things from, or dealt with in any way, were also sick and dying.

The most terrible plague ever recorded in human history—the Black Death—had begun. It raged from 1331 to 1353, moving through the entire country and killing people in enormous numbers. Although few records were kept, it appears that in 1334 alone, 5 million people died. By the time the plague was finally finished in China, some two-thirds of the population may have been wiped out—many millions!

Meanwhile, the plague was spreading westward and southward, along the trade routes on which caravans brought silks and spices to the Near East and India. Now, along with their trade goods, merchants also carried fleas, sickness, and death. An Asian writer who lived through those times tells us that millions died in India, and that Central Asia and Mesopotamia (parts of present-day Turkey, Syria, and most of Iraq) were "covered with dead bodies."

In autumn of 1347, the plague reached the city of Alexandria, Egypt. By spring of the next year it was killing as many as a thousand people a day there. It was carried up the Nile River in boats filled with people seeking to escape it. Most of them went to the great city of Cairo, which then had a population of about 500,000. During the next five months, almost 200,000 died. It became impossible to have individual funerals, and

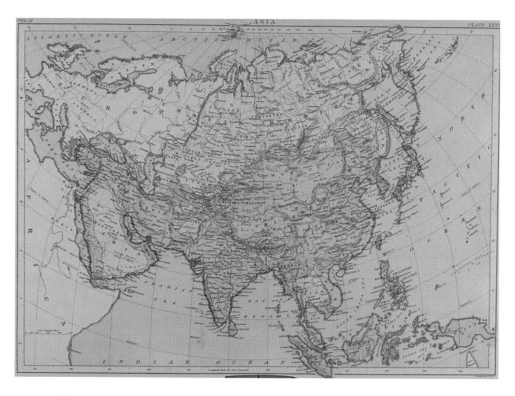

THE PLAGUE SPREAD SOUTH AND WEST ALONG THE TRADE ROUTES
FROM CHINA TO EGYPT, REACHING ALEXANDRIA IN 1347.

bodies were simply dumped by the hundreds into huge
open pits and then covered up with dirt. In time, there
were not even enough living people to bury all the dead,
and bodies were piled in mosques, public buildings, and
even shops. There were so many corpses piled up along
the sides of the roads leading out of Cairo that they
served as hiding places for robbers, who would leap out

from behind them to assault travelers trying to flee from the stricken city.

The plague spread across North Africa. "Gone is life and ease," wrote an Arab poet who lived in the city of Tunis. "There is fear and hunger and death, stirred up by the tumult and disease."

Late in 1347, some merchant ships from the Italian city of Genoa lay at anchor off one of the Near East ports where the plague was raging. As the ships rocked gently in the water, rats from the city crept aboard on gangplanks and mooring lines, and hid in dark places. Thus, the Italian ships became carriers for the sickness that had not yet reached into Europe. Once their cargoes were loaded, the ships lifted anchor and turned out into the Mediterranean Sea, heading for home, the unknowing messengers of death.

THE BLACK DEATH COMES TO EUROPE

The island of Sicily lies just off the "toe" of Italy, which is shaped like a high-heeled boot stretching down into the Mediterranean Sea. On an October day in 1347, a fleet of twelve Italian merchant ships came gliding into the harbor of Messina, one of the main port cities of Sicily. They were the ships of Genoa, returning from the Near East.

Officials of the port came onto the ships. They noticed that some of the seamen appeared to be sick. When these officials went back ashore, some of them were surely carrying fleas that had jumped to them from sick sailors. It is also a certainty that rats made their way off the ships and into the city, where they mingled with the rats of Messina.

After a while, many people in Messina were getting sick — and dying rapidly and unpleasantly. A Franciscan monk, known as Michael of Piazza, who lived in Sicily at this time and saw the sickness break out, wrote of how it affected its victims. He tells us that the first sign was severe pain that seemed to "bore" through the whole body. They then began to shiver with chills and developed raging fevers, pounding headaches, and dizziness. Eventually the sick became so weak that they could no longer stand. Pea-sized swellings, which the monk called "gland boils," appeared on their bodies: in the armpits, in the groin, or on the neck. These grew to the size of a walnut, or even a hen's egg, and caused agonizing pain. Many persons coughed or vomited

PLAGUE VICTIMS' BODIES SOMETIMES BROKE OUT WITH BLACK BLOTCHES, CAUSED BY BLEEDING UNDER THE SKIN.

THE BROWN RAT AND THE BLACK RAT — CARRIERS OF THE DEADLY PLAGUE FLEA

blood. "The sickness lasted three days," says Michael of Piazza, "and on the fourth day at the latest, the patient succumbed." Death was so certain, the monk tells us, that as soon as anyone was seized with chills and a headache, he or she sought a priest to make a confession. Then, if the person were wealthy, he would quickly make out a will!

As days went by, more and more cases of this horrifying new disease appeared, and soon it seemed as if everyone knew at least one person who had died of it. It was noticed that most of those coming down with the disease had been in contact with someone else who had already been taken by it. Obviously the disease was highly contagious. The officials of Messina were also certain that the merchant ships in the harbor had brought the sickness. The ships were ordered to leave. This was a useless move, however, because the disease was now racing through the city like wildfire.

As had happened in the cities of Asia and the Near East, there were soon more dead bodies in Messina than there were people to bury them. As had also happened in the East, people were fleeing from the sickened city in crowds. Of course, many of them had already become

MARSEILLES, LIKE OTHER PORTS IN EUROPE, HAD NO WAY TO PROTECT ITSELF FROM THE PLAGUE.

infected with the disease without knowing it. They died on the road even as they tried to escape, their bodies littering the roadside. Before dying, they usually spread the disease to others, who carried it to the places they fled to.

The large, important city of Catania lay about 50 miles (80 km) south of Messina, and by the end of

VENICE, ITALY — A BUSTLING, CROWDED MEDIEVAL CITY, WHICH PROVED THE PERFECT BREEDING GROUND FOR THE PLAGUE.

October the plague had reached there, where it raged until April of the following year. Among the thousands of Catanians who died during this time were the Duke Giovanni, who was the city's ruler, and the Patriarch Archbishop, the highest church official of the city. The plague did not play favorites; it killed rich and poor, high and low, good and bad, all with the same speed. Michael of Piazza wrote that "The town of Catania lost all its inhabitants, so that it sank into complete nothingness!" He also tells us that the plague swiftly reached all the way across the island to the town of Trapani, 160 miles (about 260 km) away from Messina, and wiped out nearly everyone living there.

As the plague flowed through Sicily it was also being carried to other parts of Europe. The ships that had been ordered out of Messina's harbor sailed for other ports. Two of them took the Black Death to the Italian port city of Pisa. There are tales of some of the other ships drifting into the French port of Marseilles, in November, with their crews lying sprawled dead on the decks. Men who went aboard these ships to investigate became unknowing hosts for fleas, which they carried back into the city.

Thus, in France as well as Italy, people soon began to die. The Black Death was now loose in Europe, and for the millions of people living there, the horror was about to begin.

A VISION OF THE PLAGUE IN FLORENCE, ITALY, BASED ON THE DESCRIPTION OF BOCCACCIO

THE SPREAD OF THE BLACK DEATH

The towns and cities of medieval Europe were cramped, crowded, and filthy. There was no sanitation, and no understanding of health care. The manure of horses and oxen lay in the streets until it was gradually washed away by rain. Garbage was simply dumped out of windows onto the streets below, providing plenty of food for the rats that swarmed everywhere. Sicknesses of all kinds were common, and doctors tried to cure them with what were basically useless magical spells. People depended mainly upon prayer and religious customs, such as making a journey to a special holy place, to protect them from disease and misfortune. Under such conditions, the plague was able to spread quickly as a city's rats became infected by the thousands and their fleas by the tens of thousands began seeking out humans.

Shortly after the ships from Messina reached Marseilles, plague erupted within the city. And again, as thousands desperately fled, the disease began to spread throughout France like oil poured from a jar. By April 1348, it reached the city of Avignon, approximately 50 miles (80 km) from Marseilles. Avignon was then the dwelling place of Pope Clement IV, head of the Roman Catholic Church, which at that time was the only Christian Church in most of Europe. There was great concern for his safety, and many urged him to flee. But his personal doctor, a man named Gui de Chauliac, told Clement to simply remain in one room of his palace, having contact with as few people as possible, until the plague had run its course. He also suggested that the pope should constantly sit, and also sleep, between two large fires, which the doctor believed would keep the air around him "purified." Although the doctor of course did not know the true cause of the disease, his advice may have actually helped his patient, because Clement survived the plague.

Others in Avignon were less fortunate, of course. It was later estimated that at least half the population died. Before the plague was finished in the town, there were some 7,000 empty houses. All their residents had died.

Throughout France, millions were dying as the Black Death marched on. In cities and towns the dead piled up with no place to bury them and no one to bury them. From his secluded room in Avignon, the pope sent out a message that he had consecrated the Rhone River, so that bodies of the dead could be thrown into it to dispose of them somehow.

In Italy, the plague spread eastward out of Pisa, reaching the cities of Bologna and Florence by April. In Florence lived the great medieval writer Giovanni Boccaccio, who survived the plague and wrote an account of it. He tells how the people of Florence "sickened by the thousands daily, and died unattended and unaided. Many died in the open street; others, dying in their houses, made their deaths known by the stink of their rotting bodies." He also tells how people were so hysterical with fear that many even refused to give any help to their own family members who had become ill. "A brother fled from his brother," he wrote. "A wife fled from her husband. What is worse, and hard to believe; fathers and mothers fled from helping their own children!" At that time, Florence had a population of around 130,000, and Boccaccio estimated that more than 100,000—about three-fourths—died during the period of plague.

Another eyewitness of the Black Death, Agnolo di Tura del Grasso, who lived in the city of Siena, wrote about what happened there. "[I]n many parts of Siena, large and deep ditches were dug for the great numbers of dead. Hundreds died day and night, and all were thrown into these pits and covered with layers of earth, so many that the pits were filled and more were dug." Like Boccaccio, Agnolo writes of how people abandoned members of their own families, even their own children, for fear of catching the plague. And he describes some ghastly sights. "[T]here were some so poorly covered with earth," he tells us, speaking of dead people, "that dogs dragged them from there and through the city, and fed on the corpses." Sadly, he relates, "[A]nd I, Agnolo di Tura, buried five of my children with my own hands."

Agnolo di Tura and others who wrote about the days of the Black Death lived through such pure horror that they didn't think people of later times, such as us, would believe what they said. "It is not possible for the human tongue to recount such a horrible thing," Agnolo wrote, "and those who did not see such horrors can well be called blessed." Another Italian writer, Petrarch, said that people of the future who read about what happened during the plague would simply think that it was all made up.

Governments did what they could to try to stop the steady spread of the plague. In the Italian city of Milan, officials ordered that any house in which someone had

THE RENOWNED POET PETRARCH SURVIVED THE PLAGUE.

INHABITANTS OF A PLAGUE-STRICKEN MEDIEVAL VILLAGE TRY TO STOP THE SPREAD OF THE DISEASE BY BURNING VICTIMS' CLOTHING.

died of the plague be boarded up. This was done even though there were still people alive in the house. Officials of the port city of Venice ordered that passengers and crewmen of ships coming into the harbor could not come ashore for forty days, until it was certain they did not have the plague. This was the origin of what we now call a "quarantine," from the Italian words *quaranta giorni,* meaning "forty days."

Despite all such efforts, the Black Death continued to spread. One of the ships that had been ordered from Messina carried the plague to Spain. From Spain it spread to Portugal. By June of 1348, the plague had crossed the Alps and moved from Italy into southern Germany. In July, a merchant ship sailing out of the French port of Calais crossed the English Channel and brought the plague to England. It spread along the coast, almost wiping out the city of Dover, and began to move inland. An English monk, Robert of Avesbury, wrote, "The plague passed most rapidly from place to place, swiftly killing ere mid-day many who in the morning had been well." Another monk reported that "very many country towns and quarters of innumerable cities are left altogether without inhabitants." The city of Norwich was an example of the ferocity with which the Black Death slashed through England. Norwich had a population of 70,000 when the plague struck and was left with only 6,628.

By November, the disease had reached into Austria and was creeping into northern Germany. In May 1349, a ship sailed from London carrying a cargo of wool to Bergen, Norway. By the time it arrived, the entire crew was dead of the plague. What had happened in Messina, Marseilles, and other places was repeated; the men who went aboard to investigate carried the sickness back into their city. The Black Death began to stalk through Norway.

PEOPLE IN BELGIUM ATTEMPTING TO BURY THE BODIES OF THE DEAD

In the summer of 1349, plague was in Belgium and Holland, and had reached the great city of Vienna, Austria. In 1350, it entered Sweden, and in the same year a ship from Norway carried it to Greenland, where it wiped out the entire population.

Except for a few small areas, the Black Death had struck every part of Europe from 1347 to 1351, when it finally came to an end. It is not known exactly how many Europeans were killed by the plague, but it was certainly many millions. The population of Europe was just about 100 million at the beginning of the plague. From investigations made at his orders, Pope Clement IV estimated that about 43 million had died—a little less than half the entire population. Today, most historians think it was actually less than that; probably from one-fourth to one-third. But in any event, it is clear that in Europe, as in Asia and Africa, the Black Death was probably the most terrible catastrophe that ever struck the human race during recorded history.

THE HORROR OF THE PLAGUE LED MANY PEOPLE TO
EMBRACE RELIGION.

IV

LIFE DURING THE PLAGUE YEARS

As Agnolo di Tura, Petrarch, and others predicted, those of us now living long after the time of the Black Death cannot really imagine what things were like then. For most people, the time of the plague was utter horror. They watched people die in the streets and saw dead bodies lying in the streets and roads. They saw corpses brought out of the houses of their neighbors and piled on wagons that went rumbling off to the pits where dead people were being thrown in by the hundreds each day. They lived with the stench of rotting bodies constantly hanging in the air they breathed. Most of them had lost loved ones to the plague, but they did not grieve about it because they fully expected to soon be dead themselves. Death could come not only from the plague, but also

DURING THE PLAGUE, MANY PRAYED TO SAINT SEBASTIAN FOR DELIVERANCE.

from starvation, for there were not enough people left in many places to do the farming and care for the livestock. Almost all the schools and universities had closed, public affairs had come to a halt, and most work had stopped. Many people felt they were seeing the end of the world—the end of all human life.

Of course, people managed as best they could, just as most people now do after a tornado or earthquake strikes. Many people turned to religion. Roman Catholic masses were still held as long as there were priests alive to conduct them. To prevent the possibility of passing the plague from one person to another, priests often gave the Host (holy bread) to people with a long spoon or even a pole, instead of putting it directly into their mouths as was usually done.

It became common for people to pick out a special saint, known as a "plague saint," to pray to for protection. The most popular was Saint Sebastian, because it was believed that the way he had died, pierced by many arrows, must have been similar to the pain of the early stages of the plague.

Some people tried to buy protection and peace-of-mind for themselves by giving large amounts of money to churches and monasteries. At times, so much was being given away that officials of the towns and cities had to pass laws to prevent people from giving away almost all they owned, leaving nothing for their families.

Just as some people turned to religion, others turned away from it, denouncing God for doing such a terrible thing as sending the plague into the world. In a popular play that was performed during the time of the Black Death, the author had one of the characters say, "Oh, thou thoroughly wicked God, if I could but lay my hands on thee, truly I would tear thee to pieces!" Many people became worshipers of Lucifer (a name for the devil), calling themselves Lucifereans, and praying to him for help against God.

A number of wealthy people attempted to simply shut themselves away from the horror all around them. They closed themselves off as best they could, often in castles or remote country homes. There they feasted, made merry, and did as they pleased, pretending that all was well.

Some of the things people did seemed almost insane. Groups would go to cemeteries at night, where they would sing and dance wildly, as if taunting the dead, or celebrating that they themselves were still alive. People would form long lines and dance through the streets of their community, sometimes until they fainted.

A great many people became Flagellants, or "whippers." These were groups of hundreds of men, women, and sometimes children, who paraded through towns and cities lashing themselves with whips. Most

FLAGELLANTS WERE WHIPPED (OR THEY WHIPPED THEMSELVES) AS A SIGN OF REPENTANCE FOR THEIR SINS. DESPITE THEIR HOPE THAT THIS EXTREME FORM OF PENANCE WOULD SAVE THEM FROM THE PLAGUE, MANY FLAGELLANTS DIED.

were common people, but sometimes nobles and priests and nuns joined the crowds. They called themselves "Brethren of the Cross," or "Crossbearers," and claimed to have received a message from heaven that the plague was a direct punishment from God for humanity's sins. The Church accused these people of teaching falsehood, and in 1349 Pope Clement sent forth a message ordering all true Christians to have nothing to do with the Flagellants. The Flagellants did not wash or keep themselves clean, and the plague easily spread among them. Eventually, many of them died, others drifted away, and the parades of chanting, singing people lashing themselves with whips were no longer seen.

The Muslim people of the Near East and Africa did not act like the Christians of Europe. Although they fled from places where the plague was raging, they did not seem to flee from family members as many Europeans did. Instead, families drew closer. But far fewer babies were born among Muslims during the plague years than among Christians. Perhaps the Muslims were reluctant to bring new lives into a world where life was being wiped out so easily.

People living at the time of the Black Death had no idea what caused diseases, so they wondered why the plague was happening. Many in Europe believed as the Flagellants did, that it was a punishment from God. Doctors, scholars, and educated people tried to find "scientific" reasons, and inasmuch as many of them believed in astrology, they felt that the plague had been caused because the planets Mars, Jupiter, and Saturn had come together in a certain part of the sky. Many doctors believed it was caused by poisonous air entering peoples' bodies through the pores of their skin. They urged people to drink vinegar to ward off the poison and to burn juniper branches in their fires so that the aromatic smoke would "purify" the air. Medieval doctors were, of course, helpless to do much of anything about the plague and died in just as great numbers as the rest of the people.

The most shocking and horrible of all the explanations given for the coming of the plague was that it had been deliberately caused by the Jewish people of Europe. Jews were generally disliked and persecuted throughout Europe in medieval times, mainly because they were believed to have been responsible for the death of Christ. As the Black Death began to move through Italy and France early in 1348, stories were spread that Jews had deliberately poisoned wells throughout Europe to cause the plague to break out among Christians. As a result, Jewish people were attacked and murdered in many places.

In Basle, a city of Switzerland, Jews were seized and forced into wooden buildings that were then set on fire. In the German city of Strasburg (now in France), 2,000

Jews were hanged. In many German towns, Jews were totally wiped out to the last man, woman, and child. Pope Clement issued a message proclaiming that the Jews were innocent of the charges being made against them. The proclamation threatened any Christian who attacked or injured Jews with excommunication (expulsion from the Church). But this did not stop the massacres, and Jews continued to be assaulted and murdered until the plague came to an end. In many places, Jewish communities ceased to exist, because their inhabitants had all been killed.

THIS WOODCUT DEPICTS JEWISH PEOPLE BEING BURNED ALIVE; MANY CHRISTIANS BELIEVED THAT THE JEWS HAD BROUGHT ABOUT THE PLAGUE.

THE BLACK DEATH WAS SO TERRIFYING THAT PEOPLE WERE
DRIVEN TO MASS DISORDER AND ACTS OF CRUELTY.

Another horror of the plague years was the danger from wild animals. There were still wolves in the forests and wilderness in much of Europe in the 1300s. They were kept in check with hunts, and were, of course, fearful of getting too close to the large numbers of humans in towns and villages. But as the populations of many communities dwindled away because of plague deaths, the wolves grew bold. There are accounts of wolves actually coming into towns in France, Italy, and Germany to seek prey. A German writer tells us that they carried off small children, and groups of them even attacked and killed men. To the people of that time, says the German, wolves "seemed no longer wild animals, but demons!"

The fourteenth century was not an easy time to live in, even without the plague. There were numerous wars, there were droughts and floods, and a great deal of hunger and sickness. But the Black Death was a terrifying, shocking experience even for the people of that century. It caused a breakdown of their civilization, and the strange and sometimes cruel events that grew out of it were the result of that breakdown.

AFTER THE PLAGUE, THE NOBLES OF EUROPE STROVE TO RETURN
TO THE GOOD LIFE. THEY ATE AT GREAT FEASTS AND DRESSED IN
DECORATIVE CLOTHING.

THE EFFECTS OF THE BLACK DEATH

When the nobles and the wealthy people throughout Europe realized that the plague was finally over, there was an explosion of rejoicing among them. Morality was ignored and overeating and drunkenness became common as people tried to forget the horror they had lived through. A medieval writer tells us that "the world began once more to live, and joy returned to it, and men began to make new clothes." New fashions in clothing did, indeed, appear at that time, featuring bright colors and tight garments that the Church regarded as sinful. Those who could afford it celebrated the end of the Black Death by overdoing all the pleasant things they could.

PEASANTS PERFORMED BACKBREAKING FARMWORK UNDER THE CONSTANT SHADOW OF THE NOBLE'S CASTLE.

But even though people were overjoyed to have survived the plague, most were terrified that it might suddenly return. They felt a desperate need for protection against it, and many turned to magic and supernatural practices as a possible way of guarding themselves. The plague did, indeed, break out again for short periods several times during the remainder of the 1300s, and people lived with constant fear of its return. They probably felt much like people of today who have been told that they may be developing a fatal disease, such as AIDS.

For the poor people—and in medieval times *most* of the people were poor—the end of the plague brought important changes. Nearly 90 percent of the people of Europe were peasants; farmworkers who were actually little better than slaves. They lived on large estates owned by nobles or high officials of the Church. Nearly all the work they did, from raising crops and livestock to grinding grain into flour, was actually done for the owner of the estate. The peasants received no pay at all, but were merely allowed to keep a small portion of the food they produced, which was often just barely enough to keep them alive. The peasants were never allowed to leave the estate and were under the complete domination of the owner, who actually thought of them as little more than animals. In fact, peasant children were called "a litter," as if they were puppies or piglets. They were not allowed to go to any kind of school, but had to begin doing work almost as soon as they could walk. Peasant families lived in crude huts and worked from dawn to dusk, every day of the week. One medieval writer likened them to fish: cold, naked, wet (from having to work in rain), and ignorant. Another said, "They lead a wretched life; poor, suffering and beggarly." However, he pointed out that without the peasants, the life of a nation would literally come apart, for it was the peasants who produced everything that was most needed: grain, meat, and material for clothing.

As the Black Death passed through Europe, millions of peasants died. As a result, things did generally come apart. People traveling through the countryside in many parts of Europe reported seeing farm fields engulfed by weeds, open and empty barns and granaries, and cattle wandering about with no one looking after them. With thousands of farms lying untended, food and other farm products became scarce and expensive.

Thus, when the plague came to an end, the surviving peasants had come to realize that they were badly needed. The owners of the great estates that had been left untended for so long were desperate to find people to work the farms again, for this was the source of the owners' wealth. In many cases, estate owners were so desperate that they even agreed to pay for help.

Many people lost faith in the power of the Church after their prayers seemed not to protect them from the plague.

Peasants found that they could go from place to place, seeking the best terms for their work. They were no longer virtually slaves; they had become wage-earners. This was a tremendous change in the way of life of most European countries; it marked the beginning of greater freedom and a better standard of living for millions of people.

The plague caused serious problems for the Church. Many people had lost faith in such things as religious pilgrimages, prayers, and special ceremonies as ways of protecting against calamity, for such things certainly had not been of any help against the plague. The Church itself had lost a large number of priests from death due to the plague and was forced to quickly replace them. But to do so, it had to make new priests out of men who were not well educated or well trained in the basic teachings of the Roman Catholic religion. Many of these men brought superstition, heresy (wrong beliefs), and poor ways of doing things into the Church. All this caused a loss of respect for the Church and for some of its teachings.

While some of the results of the Black Death were not of much significance and soon faded away, some of the effects of the plague literally shattered what had been the medieval way of life for centuries. The Church no longer had the tremendous hold over peoples' lives that it had before the Black Death, and the peasants had made a giant step toward freedom. It has been said that the Black Death brought an end to the Middle Ages and ushered in the beginning of the modern world we live in today.

A MEDIEVAL RAT CATCHER. RAT CATCHING WAS A MAJOR
OCCUPATION, BECAUSE OF THE ENORMOUS NUMBER OF RATS
SWARMING IN EVERY COMMUNITY.

THE CAUSE OF THE BLACK DEATH

Today, we refer to the plague that struck the world in the 1300s as "the Black Death," but that is actually a name that was given to it about 200 years later. The people who lived through it while it was raging most commonly called it "the Pestilence," which simply means "disease." In Europe, it was sometimes referred to as "the Italian Pestilence," probably because it had begun, for Europeans, in Italy. It was often just called "the plague."

At the time that it struck the world, the cause of the Black Death, like the cause of most diseases, was a mystery. Now, we know exactly how it is caused, and how to prevent it and cure it.

The Black Death was actually several forms of a single disease. The most common form, which caused most of the deaths during the plague years, is now known as bubonic plague. The name bubonic comes from the Latin word *bubo,* which means a swelling of one of the lymph glands in a person's neck, armpit, or groin. Bubonic plague is basically a disease of rats, caused by a bacterium (germ) that has been named *Yersina pestis* (sometimes also referred to as *Pasteurella pestis*). The bacteria infests the blood of rats and are passed to humans by the bite of fleas that generally live on rats

THIS STAMP, WHICH READS "LORD HAVE MERCY UPON US," WAS PLACED ON ENGLISH HOMES AFFECTED BY THE PLAGUE.

and feed on their blood. When a sick rat dies of the disease, its fleas seek another rat, but if none is available they will go to a human. When the flea has its first meal of human blood, it passes the bacteria into the person's bloodstream.

It takes about six days from the time a person is bitten for the symptoms of bubonic plague to appear: chills, a high fever often causing delirium, and the swelling of the lymph glands nearest to the flea bite. Next, there is bleeding under the skin that causes purplish-black blotches. This bleeding causes body cells to die and affects the person's nervous system so that he or she may jerk and twitch. The disease will kill from 50 to 60 percent of its victims within three or four days.

Another form of the disease, called pneumonic plague, strikes in a different way. Within two or three days after being bitten, the victim begins to cough, and eventually coughs and spits up blood. The coughing transmits bacteria into the air and can cause infection in anyone nearby who inhales bacteria into his or her lungs. A victim of pneumonic plague eventually goes into a coma, and in nearly all cases, dies.

The third form is called septicaemic plague. The victim breaks out with a rash within hours after the bacteria get into the body, and dies within a day, even before the swelling of the lymph glands begins. This form always causes death, but is very rare. ꙭ

The medieval writers who described the symptoms of the Black Death saw or heard of people dying from all three forms of the plague and thought the symptoms were all caused by one disease. This is why they sometimes seemed to mix up the symptoms when they described them.

The plague has been around for a long, long time. There are references in the Bible to something that occurred in the ancient Near East that sounds very much like it. It apparently swept through ancient Egypt,

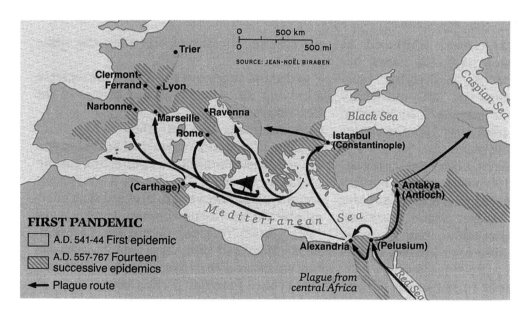

THIS MAP SHOWS THE AREAS AFFECTED BY THE PLAGUE OF A.D. 541, AS WELL AS THE MUCH LARGER AREAS RAVISHED BY LATER RECURRENCES OF THE DISEASE.

Ethiopia, and Greece, some 2,400 years ago, and there are some accounts of it appearing again, in Egypt, Libya, and Syria, about 2,000 years ago. In A.D. 262 it broke out in the Roman Empire, at one point killing 5,000 people a day in the city of Rome. About 280 years later, it struck with incredible viciousness, raging through the Eastern Roman Empire and killing millions of people in what sounds as if it might have been the worst catastrophe in human history.

The Black Death of the 1300s faded away in Europe in 1351 and appeared to be gone from Asia by 1353. But it was not completely gone; there were many rats with small amounts of bacteria lying dormant in their bodies. There were flare-ups of plague again in Europe in the 1360s and 1370s. It broke out seriously in Europe in the 1600s, and a little less seriously in the 1700s. In the mid-1800s it appeared in Egypt, Syria, Turkey, and Russia, and in 1894 it broke out on a part of the coast of China. From there, it was carried by merchant ships to India and other parts of the world. During the next twenty years, more than 10 million people died of it in India. It got to San Francisco, California, in 1900, but was quickly contained.

The bacteria that cause the plague were discovered in 1894, and in 1908 it was learned that the disease is spread by rat fleas. So, finally, in the twentieth century, medical science became able to deal with the bubonic

HUMANITY SURVIVED THE BLACK DEATH, BUT ITS CHILLING REALITY CAN STILL BE SEEN IN THE WORKS OF ARTISTS FROM THAT ERA.

plague. There was an outbreak in Vietnam in the 1960s and one in India in 1995, but it was soon brought under control. Today, especially in the western world, it is not much of a threat. However, cases of it still appear from time to time all over the world. It is carefully watched for and quickly dealt with whenever it appears. For the horrible events of the Black Death of the 1300s are well recorded in history, and are well-known throughout the world.

FOR FURTHER READING

Biel, Timothy. *The Black Death*. San Diego, CA: Lucent Books, 1989.

Bowsky, William M, ed. *The Black Death: Turning Point in History?* New York: Holt, Rinehart and Winston, 1971.

Day, James. *The Black Death*. New York: Bookwright Press, 1989.

INDEX

ABOUT THE AUTHOR

Tom McGowen, who lives in Norridge, Illinois, is the author of forty books, including several for Franklin Watts. His most recent Franklin Watts First Books are *Lonely Eagles and Buffalo Soldiers: African-Americans in World War II* and *"Go for Broke": Japanese-Americans in World War II*. In 1986, his book *Radioactivity: From the Curies to the Atomic Age* (Franklin Watts) was named an NSTA-CBC Outstanding Science Trade Book For Children. Mr. McGowen also won the 1990 Children's Reading Roundtable Award for Outstanding Contribution to the Field of Juvenile Literature.